Conversations

on

Modern Romance

Aziz Ansari

By dailyBooks

Tips for Using dailyBooks Conversation Starters:

EVERY GOOD BOOK CONTAINS A WORLD FAR DEEPER THAN the surface of its pages. The characters and their world come alive through the words on the pages, yet the characters and its world still live on. Questions herein are designed to bring us beneath the surface of the page and invite us into the world that lives on. These questions can be used to:

- Foster a deeper understanding of the book
- Promote an atmosphere of discussion for groups
- Assist in the study of the book, either individually or corporately
- Explore unseen realms of the book as never seen before

About Us:

THROUGH YEARS OF EXPERIENCE AND FIELD EXPERTISE, from newspaper featured book clubs to local library chapters, *dailyBooks* can bring your book discussion to life. Host your book party as we discuss some of today's most widely read books.

Table of Contents

Introducing *Modern Romance*

AZIZ ANSARI IS A WELL-KNOWN ACTOR AND COMEDIAN; but his book, *Modern Romance*, is not a comedy. It is a serious book with extensive research and data compilation but with the signature wittiness of Ansari. It all started when Ansari met a girl called Tanya, with whom he clicked. He invited her out to a show by sending her a text. She saw the text and did not respond at all. Ansari spent a couple of days having a complete meltdown. At this point, he realized he was behaving in a manner that was unprecedented and would never have been imaginable in the previous decades. He set out to discover how romance has changed in modern times, especially with the advent of the internet and smartphones.

He partnered with sociologist Eric Klinenberg for a research project that included focus groups with many hundreds of people in eight cities, five countries, and three continents. They decided to focus on heterosexual and middle-class people because the scope of the research would otherwise be too wide. Most of the research and the book are concentrated on the USA, but there are anecdotes and statistics from other countries as well.

Ansari discusses the various ways in which technology has transformed the way we behave and how it has changed romance for us. Without smartphones and internet, we had to wait for the person to call or meet them face to face, but now we expect instant gratification. Another point raised is how people generally settled for what was good enough, but now we expect to find our soul mate. While earlier people settled for the first person they clicked with and got married sooner, today we are ready to wait until we find the perfect person who can give us all we need in our lives. For women, the changes are even more significant because many women often got married earlier just to get out of the control of their parents, and sometimes made horrible decisions based on this. Things have definitely improved on that front. In modern times, we have what is called the "emerging adulthood," a time of transition during which both men and women try to navigate the world as adults before settling down to start families. There is also a far wider range of habitation structures today than ever before.

One of the most important things that Ansari urges on readers is to understand that the people on the other side of the phone are living, breathing, and complex people. They deserve a chance, and they definitely deserve to be treated as you would treat someone if you were talking face-to-face with them. Ultimately, he advises us to invest in people before dismissing them.

Introducing the Author

AZIZ ANSARI IS AN AMERICAN ACTOR AND COMEDIAN, most well-known for his roles as Tom Haverford in the political comedy series, *Parks & Recreation* and as Dev Shah in *Master of None*. He is also famous as a stand-up comedian and has performed shows all over the U.S. His most recent comedy special, *Live at Madison Square Garden*, was a huge hit and discussed different social issues. Like many comedians, he is a social commentator and gently brings out the different facets of social issues in a light and witty manner. Ansari is also involved in charity work and has worked with Oxfam American to encourage people to donate. He also performed a charity show to help the victims of the Boston bombing.

Ansari is of South Indian origin and belongs to a Muslim family that immigrated from Tamil Nadu to South Carolina.

Ansari himself identifies as American, atheist, and feminist. He was born in Columbia and then grew up in Bennettsville, where his family was the only non-white family in the town. He went to school in South Carolina and later went to New York University, where he majored in marketing.

Ansari began to perform stand-up comedy in New York while he was still in college. He worked on small shows and was featured by *Rolling Stone* as their choice for Hot Standup in 2005. He also won the Best Standup at HBO's Comedy Arts Festival in 2006. All this exposure and awards helped him further his career, and he landed a role in *Parks & Recreation*, which would make him a well-known face all over the country. He released his first and only book, *Modern Romance*, in June 2015. For this, he teamed up with leading sociologists to investigate the culture of dating in U.S. and around the world.

Today, Ansari is in a relationship with his pastry chef girlfriend Courtney McBroom and commutes from Los Angeles to New York on a regular basis.

Discussion Questions

. . . .

question 1

Ansari's research found that people in previous generations tended to marry within their communities, and many of them married their neighbors. Today, we no longer do so and are eager to cross boundaries of all sorts to find a soul mate. What do you think has changed (other than technology) for this to happen?

. . . .

. . . .

question 2

Women in the past often rushed into marriage to escape their parents' strictures. They often found out too late that they had married the wrong man, who was perhaps slightly more controlling than her parents. What, if any, other choices did a woman have in the earlier decades before the feminist revolution?

. . . .

. . . .

question 3

Ansari's research found that people using smartphone apps to find a date tend to be more judgmental of prospective partners. Have you ever done the same? Why do you feel compelled to not follow up on a first date?

. . . .

....

question 4

What is your overall opinion about this book? Do you find the facts presented as credible? Why or why not? What is your favorite part of the book and why?

....

. . . .

question 5

Ansari discusses different trends in dating and romance that
have changed over the years. He also discusses how different
things are in different countries. How much do you think the
prevalent culture influences peoples' dating behavior?

. . . .

. . . .

question 6

Ansari's research showed that most young people today break up
via text messages while they would prefer to be told face to face
or even by phone when the other party was initiating the
breakup. Why do you think these double standards exist?

. . . .

. . . .

question 7

In one of the anecdotes, a woman shared that she sent a sext to her boyfriend, who shared it around with his friends without her consent. Why do you think some people feel it is fine to do such a thing? Ansari calls this man "human garbage." What is your opinion of his behavior?

. . . .

· ·

question 8

One of the games people play is waiting for a certain period before responding to a text. Do you think this adds value to your experience? Why or why not?

· ·

question 9

Match.com was the first online dating portal, started in 1995. How do you think online dating has changed since then?

. . . .

question 10

When it comes to receiving messages on the internet on dating sites or apps, women receive an overwhelmingly larger number of messages as compared to men. Why do you think this is the case?

. . . .

. . . .

question 11

Ansari claims that most people are bad at online dating. Why do you think this is the case? Would these same people do better when they are introduced to people through different media? Why or why not?

. . . .

. . . .

question 12

An application like Snapchat works so that the image you send disappears after a few seconds. How do you think this is valuable to those seeking romance online?

. . . .

question 13

In Japan, the birth rate has fallen massively and due to several sociological factors, both men and women are not interested in sex or relationships. Why do you think this has happened?

· ·

question 14

In Argentina, sexual harassment of women on the streets has reached epic proportions. Why do you think this is the case? Why do you think the concept of histérica exists in Argentina? How do you think this type of molestation could be eliminated?

· ·

· ·

question 15

Marriage rates are falling globally. Why do you think this has happened?

· ·

question 16

The New York Times featured a review by Sarah Lyallin in which she claims that the book is easygoing and contains facts, advice, and comedy. Do you agree? Did you find the book both useful and entertaining?

. . . .

question 17

The review by Barbara Ellen in *The Guardian* feels that it's
refreshing to hear a contemporary male voice on the subject,
without the now predictable Pick Up Artist-style guff about
"negging," and basically browbeating and conning women into
bed. Do you agree? How different is Ansari from other modern
men who have written or talked about romance?

. . . .

question 18

In its review by John Heilpern, *Vanity Fair* claims that *Modern Romance* is adequately depicts the challenges and pitfalls of love seeking in the Digital Age. Do you consider this book a serious work? Why or why not? Does this description match the content of the book?

. . . .

· ·

question 19

NPR Books published a review by Jason Sheehan of *Modern Romance* in which it claims that what the book provides is not a series of shocking discoveries but a slow accretion of data we knew already. Do you agree? How much of the research made and the conclusions drawn from it were already known to you?

· ·

. . . .

question 20

In *The Slate*, reviewer Amanda Hess expresses her opinion that
when Klinenberg is taking his turn, and it makes for a rocky read.
Do you agree with this assessment? Can you detect which parts
were written by Ansari?

. . . .

  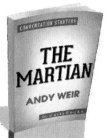

question 21

Reviewer Tyler R. Kane from *Paste Magazine* claims that most millennials will walk away from reading *Modern Romance* with an increased appreciation for those behind iPhone screens. How has your attitude towards dating and other people changed after reading this book?

question 22

Independent featured a review by Alice Jones in which the reviewer claimed that those accustomed to Ansari's stand-up may find him a little tamer in print. What differences can you find between Ansari's stand-up comedy and his book?

. . . .

question 23

The Globe and Mail compares *Modern Romance* to *Sex at Dawn* by Christopher Ryan and Cacilda Jetha. What are the similarities and differences between these two books?

. . . .

question 24

On the website *Science of Relationships*, reviewer Dr. Dyan Selterman says that while Ansari does a great job of incorporating published scientific evidence, the new information is somewhat limited. Do you agree with this? What are the limitations of the research made in this book?

· ·

question 25

Julia Felsenthal from *Vogue* claimed in her review that Ansari's book, *Modern Romance*, and his show, *Master of None*, have plenty of overlap. What is your opinion on this?

· ·

question 26

Ansari has discussed the immigrant experience in his show, *Master of None*. How do you think first generation and second generation immigrants differ in their struggles? What about the generation that comes after them?

question 27

Ansari lived in Bennettsville, South Carolina, where his was the only non-white family in the town. What kind of challenges do you think Ansari might have faced during his childhood?

question 28

Ansari is a famous stand-up comedian and is well known for his comedy specials in which he talks about current events, social issues, local culture, etc. What kind of topics make for the best comedy, in your opinion?

. . . .

. . . .

question 29

If Ansari were to write a second book, what topic would you like
to see him explore and why?

. . . .

question 30

Ansari is a famous stand-up comedian in the U.S. How would you rate his shows in comparison to other comedians?

. . . .

question 31

Today, there are many apps that help you find love. In addition, we still have the traditional methods, though the frequency of finding a mate through these methods has gone down. What would be your preferred method of finding a mate if you were looking for love today and why?

. . . .

. . . .

question 32

Ansari emphasizes how romance has changed in the last twenty years. If you were older than fifty and wanted to find a partner, would you prefer to use the traditional methods or the modern methods? Give reasons for your answer.

. . . .

. . . .

question 33

The people included in the research for this study are mostly from the middle class. If they had been from very rich or very poor families, how do you think this research might have panned out?

. . . .

question 34

In one of the anecdotes, a woman shared that she sent a sext to her boyfriend, who shared it around with his friends without her consent. If you were the target of such a person, how would you deal with the situation? If your son, brother, or male close to you did such a thing, how would it change your relationship with them?

. . . .

question 35

In the book, Ansari researched five countries: USA, France, Japan, Qatar, and Argentina. If you were doing this research, which countries would you have preferred to research and why? Which country's dating culture would you like to learn about the most and why?

. . . .

. . . .

question 36

In Japan, the birth rate has fallen massively and due to several sociological factors, both men and women are not interested in sex or relationships. The Japanese government has implemented several measures to deal with this problem. If you were in charge of the country, how would you try to fix this problem?

. . . .

. . . .

question 37

The mayor of Buenos Aires publicly claimed that he did not see why sexually harassing women was a problem. If you were a man in Buenos Aires who understood why this is a problem, how would you help change the culture to be more accepting of women's spaces and women's decisions?

. . . .

question 38

Ansari is a famous stand-up comedian and is well known for his comedy specials in which he talks about current events, social issues, local culture, etc. In this book, he discusses dating. If you were in his place, what would be your topic of choice and why?

. . . .

Quiz Questions

. . . .

question 39

Since the 1980s we have an additional phase in our lives called
_____.

. . . .

. . . .

question 40

In Japan, men masturbate into _____.

. . . .

question 41

In _____, street sexual harassment is considered normal by most men, including the mayor of the capital city.

question 42

_____ is the most popular app for gay men.

question 43

People used to settle for "good enough" in previous decades, but now they want a _____.

question 44

Ansari teamed up with sociologist _____ for this book.

question 45

Cheating is considered normal and acceptable in _____.

question 46

Ansari is a _____ by profession.

question 47

Ansari's family originally immigrated from _____.

question 48

True or false: Ansari tells us to make quick decisions when it comes to dating. True / False?

question 49

Ansari performs the role of _____ in the show, *Parks & Recreation.*

question 50

Ansari has written _____ book(s).

Quiz Answers

1. Emerging adulthood
2. Tenga
3. Argentina
4. Grindr
5. soulmate
6. Eric Klinenberg
7. France
8. Stand-up comedian
9. India
10. False; he advises us to give people a second chance and to get to know them better before crossing them out.
11. Tom Haverford
12. one

THE END

Want to promote your book group?
Register here.

Made in the USA
Middletown, DE
23 July 2023